GRAN CANARIA

250 Colour Photos

BONECHI

© Copyright by Casa Editrice Bonechi - Firenze - Italy
E-mail: bonechi@bonechi.it - Internet: www.bonechi.it

Publication created and designed by
Casa Editrice Bonechi
Editorial management: Monica Bonechi
Picture research: Marco Bonechi, Fiorella Cipolletta
Graphic design and layout: Marco Bonechi
Cover: Manuela Ranfagni
Make-up: Fiorella Cipolletta
Editing: Anna Baldini
Maps: Stefano Benini

Text by Giuliano Valdes (Editing Studio-Pisa) and Patrizia Fabbri;
Chapter "Flora" by Bruno Foggi.

Translation by Rhiannon Lewis, Christina Coster-Longman,
Helen Seale (Traduco snc di Bovone e Bulckaen, Firenze)

Photographs from the Archives of Casa Editrice Bonechi taken by
Marco Bonechi, Paolo Giambone. Pages 46 above, 47, 101 below
and for chapter "Flora": Andrea Innocenti.

Printed in Italy by
Centro Stampa Editoriale Bonechi - Sesto Fiorentino

ISBN 88-476-0280-7

* * *

The rolling dunes of Maspalomas
looking out over the distant horizon.

Introduction

The definition of the Canary Islands archipelago as being a true and proper "miniature continent", aptly sums up the morphological and climatic variety characterizing all the islands, which are clearly of volcanic origin. Clearly, since the suppositions concerning the birth of the islands, probably linked to the progressive accumulation of eruptive material from fissures in the ocean bed, are supported not only by the historical eruptions which have taken place (the most recent one was in 1971 at La Palma) and the numerous volcanic cones but, above all, by the characteristic barrancos gorges also of volcanic origin which furrow the highland and continue as far as the sea, the calderas, vast depressions of an unmistakable circular shape, and the malpaíses, desert-like typically dark-colored fields of lava.

The jagged appearance of the islands, where cliffs follow the sandy beaches and coastal plains, leading up to the characteristic central highland, is balanced by a climate which is extraordinarily mild and pleasant (temperatures of no more than 25°C in summer, generally dropping no lower than 14°C in the winter), but is also essentially quite complex. In fact, the combination of the hot Saharan winds, the warm trade winds, the humid polar sea breezes, and the cold appendage to the famous Gulf Stream, means that, just a short distance from the sunny beaches and stretches of sandy dunes, these lands which belong to Spain although they are much nearer the African continent and located at the same latitude as Florida and California, have a constant presence of clouds, the so-called "sea of clouds", covering the internal highland, where the rainfall is concentrated and where intense snowfalls can also occur above 1500 m.

These characteristics are shared by all the seven major islands (Fuerteventura, Lanzarote, Gran Canaria, La Palma, Hierro, Gomera and Tenerife) and the six smaller islands (Los Lobos, Alegranza, Graciosa, Montaña Clara, Roque del Este and Roque del Oeste) which are united under the name of the Canaries.

Gran Canaria, in particular, the central island, with a population of over 700,000 inhabitants, making up over one third of the entire population of the archipelago, is unmistakable due to its shape, which looks like an open shell surrounding the central peaks. Because of these mountain ranges of volcanic origin, which block the humid currents of the trade winds, the southernmost area of the island, where the capital Las Palmas is located, is marked by luxuriant vegetation, flanked by vast cultivated areas and banana plantations, whilst on the south side (where Maspalomas and the long sandy beaches are situated), the climate is drier, with vast stretches of dunes.

With regard to the wildlife, which has been deeply affected by the progress of mankind, this is still quite varied, although it appears to find is most characteristic representative in the unmistakable and well-loved canary.

History

The ancient and complex history of Gran Canaria has always been closely linked with that of the other islands in this splendid archipelago. Already known to the Phoenicians, Greeks and Romans, who coined elegant terms to describe their idyllic atmosphere, such as the Gardens of Hesperides and the *Fortunatae Insulae*, these strips of land, rising out of the sea beyond the mythical Columns of Hercules, represented for Plato, along with the other Macaronesian islands (Azores, Cape Verde, Madeira and Salvajes), the last traces of the legendary continent of Atlantis. Pliny the Elder refers to an expedition sent to this corner of the Atlantic by King Juba II of Mauretania, from which the explorers returned bringing their sovereign two gigantic dogs (*canes*) which were native to these islands. Tradition has it that the name of the Canaries derives from these animals.

When Juba had the islands explored, they were all – starting with Gran Canaria - inhabited by an indigenous population probably of African origin.

The fact that no mention is made of these people in Pliny's report, means that the natives were able to escape the curiosity of the foreigners by hiding in the caves.

This would have made it possible for the **Guanche** civilization, which came to the Canaries between 3000 and 2000 BC, to evolve totally autonomously for centuries, avoiding any type of external influence.

Essentially a peaceful people, who observed their own laws which were set out with extreme precision, they were also distinguished by some peculiar features both from a physical point of view (the Guanches were very tall, easily exceeding a height of 180 cm, and according to some theories, they had red hair), as well as with regard to their customs (although they lived on an archipelago, traditionally they did not know how to swim and never dedicated themselves to navigation).

Living in densely populated settlements, the Guanches practiced agriculture and sheep-farming and had a rigid social hierarchy, headed by *Guanartemes*, a sort of local chief (there were 14 just in Gran Canaria).

The god of the Sky, Alcorán was worshipped in Gran Canaria, and propitiatory ceremonies were held to favor the fertility of the land and the arrival of the rain, whilst the sacred mountains were inhabited by famous virgins like *Harimaguadas*. Women were held in great esteem because the lineage could only be perpetuated through them: in fact, future brides were taken for a period to the Cenobio de Valerón caves, used as storehouses, where they were carefully fed so that they could adequately face the important function to which they were destined.

Amongst the other peculiar customs of the Guanches, mention should be made of the practice of mummifying the bodies of the deceased. The internal organs were removed from the bodies, which were immersed for a lengthy period in saltwater and then treated with dracaena sap (this plant is native to the area), before being wrapped in goatskin. Another custom was the common practice of drilling the skull.

The Guanche civilization continued its peaceful existence until the 14th century when first the Portuguese, soon followed by the Genoese, landed on the archipelago. However, it was the 15th century, with the arrival of the Spaniards, which really marked the end of the indigenous culture of the Canaries. The populations of the other islands, troubled by internal rivalry, did not put up a very strong resistance to the conquerors, but the inhabitants of La Palma, Tenerife and, above all, Gran Canaria, behaved very differently.

In Gran Canaria, the 14 *Guanartemes* joined forces (tradition has it that this was the merit of Princess Andamana di Gáldar, who seduced them all in order to urge them to fight together) to strenuously oppose the invaders. When Gran Canaria was finally conquered and annexed to the kingdom of Ferdinand and Isabella of Spain, on April 29th 1483, by Pedro de Vera, with the help of a *Guanarteme* from the North, Tenesor Semidan, who was captured and converted, the heroic Guanche chiefs preferred death, throwing themselves off the cliffs.

The Guanche civilization was thus mortally wounded by the Spanish conquest and, within a short space of time, it literally disappeared from the Canary Islands, where precious records still remain of this ancient presence in the ruins of old dwellings, caverns and burial caves, the numerous mummies which have come to light, and the multitude of terracotta, stone and bone grave goods (there was no metal on these islands and none was imported since the Guanches did not engage in navigation), which today constitute an authentic artistic and cultural patrimony now on display at the very interesting Museo Canario in Las Palmas.

However, the Spanish conquest also radically changed the face and destiny of the archipelago, which became a compulsory port of call on route to the Americas: Christopher Columbus stopped here three times (the first time, from August 25th to September 1st 1492, during his first voyage to the New World, in order to repair the sails of the "Niña" and the rudder of the "Pinta").

Between the end of the 15th century and during the first half of the 16th century, the Portuguese introduced the first sugar cane plantations and imported the first slaves from Africa. Between the 17th and 19th centuries, many English people also settled here, importing wine and cochineal from the Canaries and introducing the cultivation of bananas, tomatoes and potatoes, destined to become the island population's main foodstuffs alongside the traditional *gofio* (toasted cornflour).

In time, the economy of the Canaries underwent a progressive and unstoppable growth, the first crowning achievement of which was, in the middle of the 19th century, the recognition of free port jurisdiction and the arrival of the first tourists. In the meantime, the population continued to assume an increasingly cosmopolitan appearance, as befitted an authentic crossroads between continents. However, the destiny of these islands, where a particular dialect is spoken which is fundamentally different from Spanish (perhaps the final legacy of the language spoken by the Guanches, probably of Berber origin), was and still is linked to Spain: divided into the two provinces of Las Palmas de Gran Canaria (which includes Gran Canaria, Lanzarote and Fuerteventura) and Santa Cruz de Tenerife (Tenerife, La Palma, Gomera and Hierro), the archipelago where, on July 18th 1936, General Francisco Franco announced his military coup with the "Comunicado de Las Palmas", is still today a region of Spain, although it has enjoyed relative autonomy since 1983.

The main resources of the archipelago's economy are linked to agriculture, animal rearing and fishing (the surrounding waters are extraordinarily abundant with fish), but of significantly greater importance is tourism, a resource which, in recent years, has turned out to be the true treasure of the Islands of Eternal Spring.

According to Pliny, in ancient times the Canaries were inhabited by gigantic dogs from which the name of the islands is derived.

Cenobio de Valerón, a view of the interesting caves once inhabited by the Guanche civilization.

The sandy shore of Las Palmas and one of the splendid seafront boulevards, crowded at promenade time.

The lights and reflections create a magical night-time atmosphere along the picturesque promenade of Playa de las Canteras.

LAS PALMAS

For those who approach **Gran Canaria** by boat, the island looks like a beautiful shell emerging from the maritime depths of the Atlantic. Known locally as the *"isla redonda"* due to its circular shape, it is an enormous mass of rocks, the highest point being Pozo de las Nieves (1949 m). This volcanic island, characterized by precipitous deep valleys *("barrancos"),* volcanic cones and craters which create a picturesque landscape, rich in contrast is made up of two large regions: the so-called *"Isla Nueva"* region in the northeast, which is a fertile green area of more recent geological formation and the *"Isla Vieja"* region in the south-east, of much earlier morphological formation, which is an arid bleak area characterized by vast expanses of dunes situated along its coastline.

The city of **Las Palmas** is situated in the north-eastern quadrant of the island and stretches out along the isthmus comprised between the beaches of Las Canteras and Las Alcaravaneras as far as the mountainous promontory known as *"La Isleta"*. Las Palmas is the provincial capital of Gran Canaria which also includes the islands of Fuerteventura and Lanzarote. Although it is characterized by modern buildings, it is nevertheless a picturesque city, rich in architectural contrast, colors and surroundings. It is frequently visited by a cosmopolitan assortment of tourists and is bordered by vast, beautiful beaches, which,

together with numerous others along the coast, have led to the island being known as the "Island of the Golden Sands". Thanks to the distinct advantages conferred upon it by a pleasant microclimate and the wide range of tourist and accommodation facilities on offer, the city has become one of the major centers of attraction of the whole archipelago and is an important port of call along air and shipping routes.

The origins of Las Palmas date back to 1478, the year in which the Spanish conqueror Juan Rejón landed on the island. He built the military quarters known as the "Real de Las Palmas" near the deep valley of Guinigada. Later, Pedro de Vera successfully established definitive rule over the island in 1483. At the beginning of the following century, Las Palmas gradually took on the dimensions of a large city, as a consequence of considerable building work carried out in the districts of Triana and Vegueta. The increasing importance of the town, in both administrative and commercial fields, resulted in its being attacked by English, French, Dutch and Barbaric pirates. Unfortunately, the destruction of the city, at the hands of Peter Van der Does, is a well-known episode in the history of Las Palmas. During the time of the voyages of Columbus, the port of Las Palmas became one of the principal ports of call along the shipping route, which the famous Genoese navigator maintained led to the Indies.

The Port

To give an idea of the importance of this maritime port, it would be sufficient to say that the *Puerto de la Luz* at Las Palmas de Gran Canaria, is regarded as the most important Spanish port. Due to its geographical position, which makes it vitally important for world trade routes, it acts as a link between the Old and New World. The construction of the port, along the isthmus of Guanartene, began in the 19th century, and was based upon plans drawn up by the engineer Juan Léon y Castillo. Its construction was yet another contributing factor to the growth of the city. Along the spacious wharves of *La Luz, Santa Catalina* and *Pesquero* many boats, oil tankers and cargo vessels are berthed, while numerous fishing boats stop off here after successfully venturing out into the waters of the Atlantic Ocean.

On the previous pages:
a marvelous panoramic view of the city of Las Palmas.

Some attractive views of the tourist port of Las Palmas, crowded with all types of craft.

Castillo de la Luz

The castle, overlooking the port buildings situated along the *Wharf of Pesquero*, was built at the turn of the 15th century in answer to the specific need of providing the city with a secure defensive system: the incessant pirate raids led to the construction of this fortified structure, which served as a means of defense and also discouraged further pirate attacks. Restoration work, under the auspices of the Administrative Department of Fine Arts, was carried out during the 1970s. The castle is an imposing building, built of enormous square stone blocks and has a square-shaped plan, reinforced by corner towers (one of which has a curious conical roof).

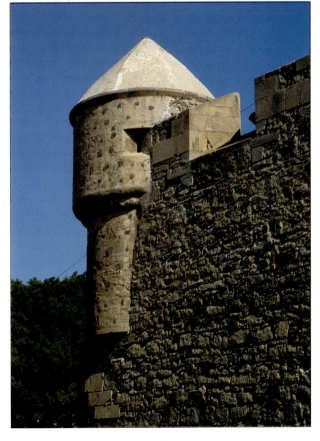

The mighty fortified structures of the majestic Castillo de la Luz, opposite the Pesquero wharf.

Playa de las Canteras

At Las Canteras, the long stretch of sea-front borders the western side of the isthmus which connects the most densely populated part of the city with the mountainous promontory of *La Isleta*. The long, wide beach, of fine ochre-colored sand, has led to the whole of the Gran Canaria being known as "the island of the golden sands". The sands slope gently down towards the azure waters of the ocean. Here the water is particularly safe for bathing because of the presence of a natural dam formed by rocks.

The vast and splendid Playa de las Canteras.

Along the sea-front, the entire skyline is taken up by the modern and comfortable first class hotels. The hotels, restaurants, local shops and entertainment facilities overlook the enchanting tree-lined avenue which runs along the sea-front. Because of the pleasant, sunny and inviting climate and the large number of tourists who frequently visit the island, the beach of Las Canteras and its neighboring avenues are always crowded with people from all over the world, thus giving the main town of the Canary Islands the image of a small cosmopolitan capital.

Parque de Santa Catalina

Not far from the wharf of Santa Catalina, in the center of the residential nucleus which lies between the wide sandy beaches of Las Canteras and Las Alcaravaneras, stands the square surrounded by trees in which the **Park of Santa Catalina** is situated. The luxuriant palm trees together with the dense and abundant vegetation of the gardens, create a decidedly tropical atmosphere. The piazza is bordered on all sides by modern constructions built of cement and glass. The elegant **Tourist Office** with its bold architectural lines, stands out from the other buildings in the square. Its unmistakable, cylindrical structure dominates the center of Las Palmas, the port, and the coastal district. In fact, the Park of Santa Catalina is both the commercial and shopping center of Las Palmas, and is the place where one can buy the typical products of the provincial capital. Until late in the night it is always full of tourists and visitors of all nationalities.

The luxuriant Parque de Santa Catalina, dominated by the cylindrical shape of the Casa del Turismo.

Parque Doramas

This green public park is situated in one of the districts of Las Palmas which is characterized by the delightful features of a "garden-city". In addition to the famous palm trees, which are almost a kind of "living symbol" of this enchanting city, the Doramas Park contains much exuberant and lush tropical vegetation. The cactus plants, the exotic species and the typical flora of the Canaries provide an undoubtedly decorative aspect to the city.

Behind these beautiful gardens stands the **Hotel Santa Catalina**. The architectural elegance of the building can be attributed to its designer: Miguel Martín Fernández de la Torre, the brother of the more famous Néstor.

Some pictures of the verdant Parque Doramas, where the Hotel Santa Catalina stands in all its elegance.

Pueblo Canario
Museo de Néstor

The so-called **Pueblo Canario** is one of the most typical and characteristic parts of the town, and is reached by passing under a large monumental arch upon which can be seen the coat of arms of the town which bears the inscription *"Segura tiene La Palma"*. The construction of this enchanting architectural complex, set around a large courtyard, in keeping with the traditional building style of the constructions of Las Palmas, was the inspiration of the famous local painter, Néstor Martín Fernández de la Torre. The project was carried out by the painter's brother, Miguel. In the tree-lined courtyard, decorated with lush tropical vegetation, many enjoyable traditional events are held, while typical local products and handicrafts can be bought in the nearby shops and stores. Contained within this complex is the **Museo de Néstor**, where a vast collection of the works of the artist who lived here during the 19th and 20th centuries are on show (e.g. etchings, oil paintings and self-portraits). Worthy of note are the *Poema de la Tierra* and the *Poema del Mar*.

Another view of the characteristic Parque Doramas.

The entrance arch into Pueblo Canario and, below, the Museo de Néstor.

17

"El Bodegón"

Amongst the many attractions offered by Pueblo Canario, the elegant folk group displays should not be missed. Dressed in their charming local costumes, these groups give exhibitions of the island's traditional dances. Delightful and enthralling entertainment for tourists who, after watching the dancing, can also visit the wonderful restaurant, which is an integral part of the Pueblo itself. Called the "Bodegón", this is a characteristic venue with a renowned cuisine, behind which is an area that used to house a mini-zoo and is now the favorite retreat of a pair of turtles.

Pueblo Canario always offers tourists a festive atmosphere, with groups of young people wearing traditional costumes giving displays of the local dances accompanied by the music of a picturesque band.

The characteristic Art Nouveau gazebo which can be admired in the Parque San Telmo.

Parque San Telmo

In the ancient heart of Las Palmas stretches a small but very pleasant green oasis, the Parque San Telmo, famous mainly for its characteristic Art Nouveau **gazebo**. In front of this gazebo are the barracks where, on July 18th 1936, General Francisco Franco announced his military coup to the country.

Calle Mayor

In the southern part of Las Palmas, in the characteristic **Triana** quarter which, with the **Vegueta** (literally "small prairie", the old quarter, an authentic web of traditional architecture) constitutes the so-called *Ciudad Real de Las Palmas*, the first Spanish nucleus of the city, runs the Calle Mayor, one of the main commercial streets of the island's capital. Transformed into a pedestrian precinct, the numerous typical and traditional shops have made this a popular shopping area, also distinguished by the elegance of the imposing buildings which overlook it.

A picture of the Calle Mayor de Triana, pedestrian oasis and authentic commercial heart of the city.

Home-Museum of Benito Pérez Galdós

In addition to the characteristic shops on the Calle Mayor, the Triana quarter also hosts the house where Benito Pérez Galdós, the famous writer and true local glory, was born. The author of novels clearly inspired by the realistic style of Balzac, like "Fortunata y Jacinta", "Nazarín" and "Tristana", was born in 1843. Also penned by the man who is considered to be one of the greatest Spanish writers of all time (the director Buñuel has often been inspired by his works), are 46 volumes of "National Events", a detailed account of Spanish history from 1805 to 1873. Las Palmas has always been deeply proud of its famous son, who actually lived for a long time in Santander, in the north of the Iberian peninsula, and his modest home at number 6 Calle Cano, where he was born and lived until 1863, has been turned into a **museum**. Here it is possible to admire numerous objects which belonged to the writer, as well as ancient editions of his works. The city has also named a **theater** after Pérez Galdós, which was built in 1919 near the cathedral and can seat an audience of 1400.

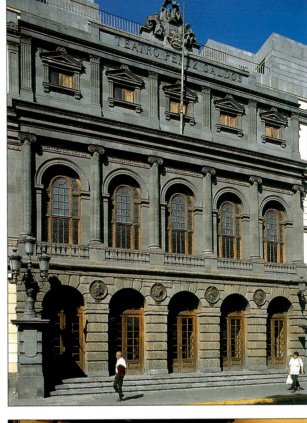

The elaborate façade of the Teatro Pérez Galdós.

Some views of the interior of the house where the great writer was born, now transformed into a museum.

Casa de Colón

One of the major tourist attractions of Las Palmas de Gran Canaria is, without doubt, the **House of Christopher Columbus**. This white building with its characteristic Spanish features has two covered wooden balconies in the upper part of its façade which jut out from the main body of the building. The main entrance door in the center of the façade is particularly worthy of note. Above is situated a charming small window enhanced by a wealth of ornamental motifs. Over these can be seen a decorative coat of arms. The house dates back to the 15th century but later underwent several transformations. This building was (at least until the beginning of the 16th century) the home of the military governor of Gran Canaria.

The origins of the present name of the house can be traced back to the time when the famous Genoese navigator stopped here on his voyage towards the New World to visit his friend, Antonio de Torres, the governor of Gran Canaria. It is a well-known fact that Columbus made frequent use of the landing places on the Canary Islands during his transoceanic voyages due to the natural logistics of the islands and to the particularly favorable seafaring conditions found at these latitudes.

The marvelous rear façade of the so-called House of Christopher Columbus, in Las Palmas. With its elegant and elaborate portal, it has a charming fountain situated opposite it.

Another detail of the decorations on the portal of the rear façade of the Casa de Colón.

According to reliable historical sources, during Columbus' first voyage, the rudder of the "Pinta" broke while he was sailing past the island of Lanzarote and so the Genoese admiral was forced to land at the port of San Sebastián on the island of Gomera. This same port became one of Columbus' favorite landing places during his later voyages. During his fourth voyage, the discoverer of the New World stopped at the port of Las Palmas to visit his friend, the above-mentioned governor, Antonio de Torres.

The outer courtyard *(Patio des Armas)* is characterized by a beautiful 16th century *cloister* which clearly shows the salient features of Renaissance architecture. Among the most interesting artistic elements to be seen here are a charming, elaborately decorated Gothic window and a remarkable *well*, which betrays the characteristic features of the Gothic style and dates back to the late 16th century. The inner courtyard, surmounted by a gallery which is sustained by columns and numerous wooden beams immediately catches the visitor's eye due to the presence of some ancient cannons and the rich decorative effect created by the numerous green plants and small trees on display.

The **interior** of the building houses several interesting museums; worthy of note are the **Museum of Fine Arts**, the **Columbus Museum** and the **Historical Archives of the Province**. Particularly worthy of note is the collection of paintings which includes some excellent canvases painted by past and contemporary painters. The collection includes works by Veronese, Guido Reni, Guercino, Meléndez, Morales, Lucas and Esquivel. Several paintings have been brought here from the *Prado Museum* in Madrid.

The charming main façade of the building and, on the right, three views of the Patio des Armas, embellished with a beautiful 16th century well.

The rich and very interesting Museo Colombiano, with models of the famous caravels.

Among the numerous sculptures, bronze sculptures and clay reliefs, is an outstanding valuable representation of *Christ* done by Luján Pérez. In their entirety, the collections on show at the Casa de Colón give us an interesting insight into the history and civilization of the archipelago (there are numerous exhibits belonging to the Guanche civilization), and here it is also possible to see ancient nautical maps and instruments, models of the sailing ships of Columbus, prototypes of ancient mills where "gofio" was made ("gofio" was a flour obtained from toasted maize and formed part of the staple diet of the Guanche population), a valuable 16th century baptismal font, which originates from S. María de Guía and collections of tapestries from Majorca, period furniture, furnishings, porcelain and ancient documents and medals.

The rear of the building, overlooking the quiet *Plaza del Pilar Nuevo* is also worthy of note. Here one can admire a delightful polygonal-shaped fountain. The most outstanding artistic feature is the beautiful Gothic portal set in a large ornamental frame which is characterized by the presence of extremely refined bas-reliefs.

In the immediate vicinity of the Casa de Colón stands the so-called **Ermita de San Antonio Abad**. This charming small 17th century church is characterized by the slender bell-tower which rises up from the façade. In the interior is a remarkable main altar. This 17th century church (constructed on the site of a previous 15th century place of worship, acting for a long time as the cathedral of Las Palmas) is of particular interest, as it was here, in this very church, that Christopher Columbus took part in a mass before setting sail on his first memorable voyage towards the New World.

An ancient coat of arms preserved in the Casa de Colón.

One of the most characteristic moments of a visit to the Museo Colombiano.

The imposing façade of the Catedral de Santa Ana, clearly inspired by the neo-classic style, and a detail of one of the twin towers.

Opposite page, another detail of the cathedral's façade and a picture of the bronze dogs on guard in the square opposite, a reminder of the canes to which the Canary Islands owe their name.

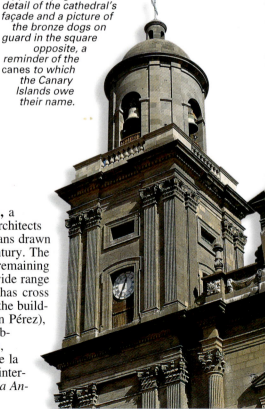

Catedral de Santa Ana

At Las Palmas, tourists can also admire the **Cathedral of Saint Anna,** a building of considerable architectural interest as a result of the numerous architects who worked upon its construction. Work on the building, based on the plans drawn up by Diego Alonso de Motaude, was initiated at the turn of the 15th century. The building which we see today was finished in 1875, once work on the last remaining southern tower had been completed. Although the cathedral is built in a wide range of architectural styles, the tripartite division of the interior, which also has cross vaulting, is clearly of strong Gothic influence. The façade and the rear of the building (the former being flanked by two identical towers, designed by Luján Pérez), are evidently built in the Neoclassical style. In the interior, many gold objects used for religious functions can be seen (e.g. processional crucifixes, chalices and candelabra) together with some fine paintings by Rodriguez de la Oliva, Cristóbal Hernández de Quintana, Juan de Roelas, as well as some interesting sculptures (e.g., *Virgen del Pino* - 18th century, *Nuestra Señora de la Antigua*, *San Pedro* - 17th century, and various other works).

Diocesan Museum of Sacred Art

A door on the eastern side of the splendid cathedral gives access to the small but very interesting Diocesan Museum of Sacred Art, created in 1984 with the help of private donations, and today a precious artistic complement to the adjoining religious building, where its **Treasures** are preserved. In fact, in the museum it is possible to admire a rich collection of valuable liturgical objects, made with elegant skill, sculptures and enchanting creations of Spanish colonial art in general and of the Canaries in particular, as well as parchments, ancient manuscripts and a large number of goldsmith's products, adorned with precious stones of inestimable worth.

The slender Gothic naves, with cross vaults, in the cathedral.

The interesting Diocesan Museum, where the precious Tesoro de la Catedral de Santa Ana is preserved.

Plaza del Cairasco

Between the historical Vegueta quarter, a matchless gallery of traditional architectural styles and characteristic buildings, and the Triana area, is the Plaza del Cairasco, with its pleasant central green flowerbed dominated by the bust of Cairasco which gives the square its name. Some particularly noteworthy buildings overlook the square: the *Hotel Madrid*, the only hotel in the ancient quarter of Las Palmas which, amongst other things, has a very pleasant terrace bar; and, most importantly, the magnificent **Gabinete Literario**, with its unmistakable and richly eclectic style.

Typical Canary-style architecture, with the unique framed windows and graceful wooden balcony.

An example of the mighty fortifications which still today remind us of the pirate raids carried out in Las Palmas in the past.

The elegant front of the Gabinete Literario, which dominates Plaza del Cairasco.

Typical Features of the Northern Side of the Island

F or those who are not content with just lazing around or basking in the sun on one of the "golden" beaches of Gran Canaria, the northern side of the island offers many interesting landscapes and environments for those tourists who wish to explore the place in greater detail. Taking the road which runs through the fertile agricultural regions of Gran Canaria *("autopista norte"* the north motorway), the visitor's attention is immediately drawn by the vast expanses of banana plantations. These, to a lesser extent, can also be found along the more barren southern coasts, and produce splendid fruit which constitutes the flagship of the agricultural produce of the island, which is largely destined for export. In other places, one can enjoy the enchanting views of the wild and rugged coastline with picturesque villages dotted along it.

Ordinary views of Gran Canaria: luxuriant banana plantations.

A picturesque glimpse of the charming seaside village of San Felipe; a hazardous viaduct of the "autopista norte" crossing a deep valley.

A view of the marvelous cathedral of Arucas.

A charming glimpse of the slender Gothic towers overlooking the cathedral.

ARUCAS

Arucas is the third most highly populated center of the archipelago. This idyllic setting is created by the dazzling brightness of its white houses which are in sharp contrast with the dark profile of its turreted Cathedral. Situated on the northern slope of the island, and dominating the fertile agricultural region which is located between the precipitous deep valleys of San Andrés and Tenoya, this enchanting rural village (which is almost the size of a town) is characterized by the typical architectural features of the island. The wide use of a particular type of stone (mined from a nearby quarry), used in the construction of its buildings, helps to create a graceful, decorative effect. Surrounding the town are the vast banana plantations which stretch out as far as the eye can see. These constitute the town's main source of economic wealth, which was once based on the cultivation of sugar cane and the rearing of the cochineal beetle (from which red food coloring is obtained).

The main tourist attraction of the town is the **Cathedral**, a building of great architectural value, which was completed between 1909 and 1917. The construction, which is built in the manner of the ancient Gothic cathedrals, is characterized by its dark volcanic stonework and dominated by slender towers and pointed spires. The main feature of the façade is the splayed portal surmounted by a charming series of blind arches and a rose window. In the well-proportioned interior some works of considerable artistic merit can be seen, the most outstanding of which being a valuable sculpture by the local sculptor Manuel Ramos entitled *Cristo Yacente*. Finally, the excursion to the panoramic summit of the **Montaña de Arucas**, situated just outside the town, is well worth making.

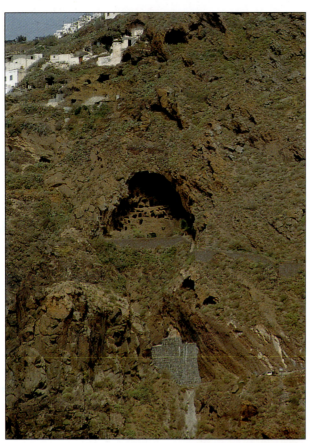

CENOBIO DE VALERÓN

The so-called Cenobio de Valerón, situated in close proximity to the rocky *Cuesta de Silva*, provides substantial evidence of the existence, on the island, of the ancient Guanches civilization. This fascinating network of grottos - there are almost 350 - opens out in the interior of a rocky lava cavity, set in the mountainside and surrounded by lush abundant vegetation. This inextricable maze of underground communicating passages recalls the troglodytic dwellings carved out of the rock. According to some experts, the Guanches probably lived and stored their food supplies here because of the favorable conditions of humidity and temperature. On the other hand, others believe that here lie the remains of an ancient Guanche sanctuary, where the high priestess - known as "harimaguadas" – instructed the young maidens before their marriage ceremonies.

*Following pages:
the unique profile of the Montaña de Gáldar, at whose
feet lie the ancient rival towns of Guía and Gáldar.*

*These pages: the famous Cenobio de Valerón, a dense
network of caves which constitutes one of the most
complex records of the Guanche civilization to reach
the present day.*

GUÍA

Resting between vast banana and sugar cane plantations, stretching as far as the cliffs of *Punta Guanarteme*, Guía (Santa María de Guía to give its full name), is an ancient village, now famous for its renowned cheeses (*quesos en flor*), but in the past divided by its bitter rivalry with neighboring Gáldar. The *main church* is particularly interesting, excellently refined by the works of sculptor Luján Pérez, who was born in Guía in 1756.
Just a few kilometers away are the famous *Cenobio de Valerón* caves.

GÁLDAR

At the foot of the *Montaña de Gáldar*, also called the "miniature Teide" due to its similarity to the volcano of Tenerife, just a short distance away from long, beautiful beaches of black sand and pebbles, the pre-Hispanic capital of Gran Canaria, Gáldar, is today a pleasant town which rises on the dark lavic land from which enormous blocks of pumice stone are still extracted today. In addition to the interesting architectural style of the *Town Hall* and the 15th century church of *Santiago de los Caballeros*, which has an elegant baptismal font in green Seville ceramic, traditionally used to baptize the descendants of the last king of the Guanches, the town is best known for the neighboring **Gruta Pintada**, a Guanche cave discovered in 1881, on the walls of which geometric black and ochre paintings are preserved, the only polychromes of the whole archipelago.
Also near Gáldar is the interesting necropolis called **Túmulo de la Guancha**, which has recently been restored and opened to the public.

The elegant neo-classic church of Gáldar.

Views of the neighboring Cuevas de las Cruces, with the characteristic caves (below) hollowed out of lavic rock.

The charming rocky coast near Puerto de las Nieves, with the characteristic cliff renamed "Dedo de Dios" (below).

Some views of the seaside village of Puerto de las Nieves, a busy fishing port.

PUERTO DE LAS NIEVES

Puerto de las Nieves is the port of **Agaete**, a pretty village set out along a green terraced slope, at the foot of a steep mountain. The port of this seaside village and fishing center is quite an important one, due to its sea links with the island of Tenerife and the major role it plays in the exportation of bananas.

The wide expanses of pebbly beaches, situated beyond the village, are one of the outstanding features of the landscape. The precipitous, steep cliffs along the high and rocky coastline, tower over the blue and inviting waters of the sea, which constitute an irresistible temptation for swimmers. In the background, opposite the steep rock-face which juts out over the sea, rises the curious outline of the **Cliff of Partido**, a gigantic monolith silhouetted against the sky, which is probably the reason why it is also known locally as *"El dedo de Dios"*.

JARDÍN CANARIO

Moving towards the peak of the island, surrounded by breathtaking views and fascinating nature, it is a good idea to stop and admire the luxuriant Jardín Canario, a true paradise for local flora, created thanks to the passionate determination of a Swedish botanist, dominated by splendid examples of dracaenas, majestic cactuses and numerous species of Canary Island plants. It is undoubtedly an enthralling experience which can be pleasantly extended to include a visit to the restaurant of the same name ("Jardín Canario"), where it is possible to enjoy the delightful view and savor the simple and tasty dishes of the island's cuisine.

Some eloquent pictures of the luxuriant vegetation characterizing the marvelous Jardín Canario, in its verdant natural setting, just a few kilometers from Las Palmas. Left, the "Mato Risco" with its purple flowers; right, the "Cardon", a plant which is typical of the dry habitat of the Canaries.

SAN MATEO

Situated at a height of over 800 m and surrounded by a crown of imposing mountains and vast plantations of cereals and pulse vegetables, the picturesque alpine village of San Mateo, south of Las Palmas, on the slopes of the Pozo de las Nieves, is the ideal starting point for delightful mountain hikes along footpaths entering a natural environment of rare and stimulating beauty. In San Mateo, it is definitely worth paying a visit to the *Casa Museo de Cho Zacarías*, a sort of museum of peasant traditions, where it is possible to admire agricultural equipment, tools, Canary Island knives, ceramics and many other objects linked to the rural tradition of this land. Nearby is the *Church of La Laguneta*, flanked by two bell-towers.

CALDERA DE BANDAMA

This charming natural amphitheater is formed from the crater of an ancient dormant volcano. From the top of the edge of the crater one can enjoy an exceptional view of the surrounding landscape. Nearby is a well-equipped and popular golf course.

San Mateo, the monument dedicated to workers; the impressive crater of Caldera de Bandama, still easily recognizable.

The picturesque alpine village of San Mateo, on the slopes of Pozo de las Nieves, famous for its museum (below) dedicated to peasant traditions.

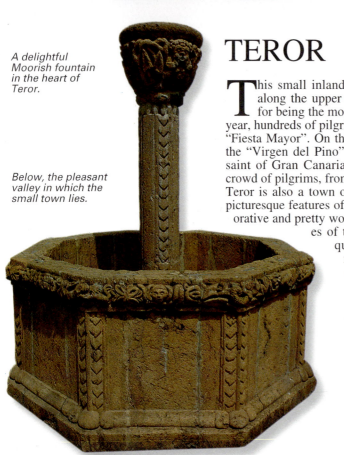

A delightful Moorish fountain in the heart of Teror.

Below, the pleasant valley in which the small town lies.

TEROR

This small inland town is situated in a pleasant geographical position along the upper margin of the valley of Tenoya. The place is famous for being the most important religious center of Gran Canaria and every year, hundreds of pilgrims flock to Teror, especially on 8th September, for the "Fiesta Mayor". On this day, the celebrations which take place in honour of the "Virgen del Pino" (literally, the Madonna of the Pine-tree - the patron saint of Gran Canaria) culminate in an impressive procession in which a crowd of pilgrims, from all over the island, take part.

Teror is also a town of great architectural interest, as can be seen from the picturesque features of the small white houses with their stone walls and decorative and pretty wooden balconies. The typical characteristics of the houses of the nobility, together with the peace and serene tranquillity of this small well-kept town, invites even the most hasty of tourists to stop and contemplate the natural beauty of this spot.

Teror, the typical stone dwellings with their artistic small wooden balconies.

A view of the quiet square overlooked by the Town Hall (Ayuntamiento) a building of great architectural merit.

Teror, the façade embellished by a wooden balcony (top left), the characteristic wooden portico with central fountain and floral ornaments (below), and two interior views of the famous Casa Museo Patronos de la Virgen.

Basílica de la Virgen del Pino

The basilica which we see today, stands on the site of a pre-existent 16th century church. The reason why churches were built on this spot dates back to 1481, when it was said that on this spot, the Madonna appeared among the branches of a pine tree. The building of the present church (based on the plans drawn up by Antonio Lorenzo de la Rocha) was completed in 1767. The features of the basilica are reminiscent of the Neo-classical style, while the nave and the two aisles of the interior betray evident Baroque features. Mention should also be made of the elegant octagonal Gothic bell-tower which has features reminiscent of Portuguese architecture. The most valuable artistic work to be seen here is the 15th century sacred effigy of *Nuestra Señora del Pino* which is lavishly decorated with valuable jewels and which, from the top of the main altar, dominates the interior of the church. Among the sculptures done by the local artist José Luján Pérez, mention should be made of *El Cristo de la Columna*.

The simple but imposing Basílica de la Virgen del Pino, in Teror. This is flanked by a slender octagonal-design Gothic bell-tower.

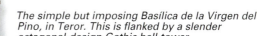

54

BALCÓN
DE ZAMORA

One of the obligatory stops along the road which leads from Teror to Valleseco is Balcón de Zamora. From this splendid panoramic belvedere the tourist can admire one of the most enchanting views over the picturesque valley of Teror and its surrounding mountains.

Teror, the simple but attractive façade of the Basílica de la Virgen del Pino with, below, a picture of the rich baroque interior and the revered image of Nuestra Señora del Pino, patron saint of Gran Canaria.

From Balcón de Zamora (above), on the road to Valleseco, it is possible to enjoy one of the most splendid and panoramic views of the small town of Teror and its green valley.

The characteristic green stone cross and, behind it, the famous Parador Nacional, the two main attractions of Cruz de Tejeda.

CRUZ DE TEJEDA

This splendid panoramic belvedere gets its name from a strange **cross** made of green stones which stands in the center of the island, exactly opposite the **"Parador Nacional"** which has the same name. The latter is a large hotel situated at the foot of a bare and rough rock-face. Here the landscape is full of curious and fascinating features; on exceptionally clear days one can see as far as the top of Teide, 3718 m, the highest summit of the archipelago (on the island of Tenerife) which is permanently covered with snow. The surrounding mountains are characterized by their rugged and rocky features and it is for this reason that here the landscape resembles the surface of the moon. Dominating a deep gorge stands the monolithic outline of the *Roque Nublo* which, together with the *Roque Bentayga* and the *Roque Fraile*, confer an atmosphere of a "petrified forest" as Miguel de Unamuno aptly defined this sight.

One of the imposing needles of rock which make up the summit of Roque Nublo and the highest peaks of the mountainous heart of Gran Canaria.

The great mountains

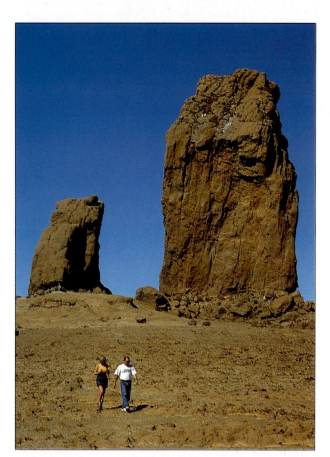

When our thoughts turn to the Canary Islands, the images which most immediately spring to mind are of sun, sea and long sandy beaches. But this archipelago can offer the somewhat surprised visitor something very different: for example, a mountainous core which is a feature common to a large part of the islands. Gran Canaria can also boast this morphological peculiarity: in fact, steep and harsh rocky peaks rise up from the center of the island, contributing to producing an image inconsistent with the one commonly associated with this island. The ancient Guanches used to worship the great needles of rock which rise towards the sky until they disappear into the sea of clouds, and the whole mountain area was considered sacred.

Here and following pages:
some more pictures of Roque Nublo and the other mountains which make up the central massif of the island. The slopes of the Canary Island peaks are covered with thick pine forests, but above a certain altitude, they are dominated by rock alone, against a background of enchanting and superb views, often partially hidden by the characteristic sea of clouds.

This land, situated at an altitude of over 1000 m, difficult to cultivate without resorting to terracing, has always been identified by the island's inhabitants with the general name of *cumbre*, summit, which, in its succinct eloquence, fully mirrors the characteristics of the area. In fact, around the tops of *Pozo de las Nieves* (1949 m), *Moriscos* (1771 m) and *Roque Nublo* (1700 m), there is a flourish of summits and peaks, from *Roque Bentayga* to *Roque Fraile* and *Cruz de Tejeda*. On their slopes, pasture land and orchards alternate with remote villages, whose inhabitants proudly lead their difficult lives, the only kind permitted by the harsh nature of these lands, to which they seem so closely tied.

As the altitude increases, the sporadic cultivated fields are replaced by large green pine forests, a thick crown which covers the slopes and acts as a prelude to the most spectacular part of this central massif: the vast, steep, rugged, deserted rocky crest. This authentic, phantasmagoric stone kingdom can only be reached by steep pathways winding through the stony terrain, only recommended for mules and the more enterprising and well-equipped cross-country vehicles.

Deep valleys, imperious peaks, green conifers and, here and there, a veil of clouds: these are the most typical elements characterizing the stupendous cumbre *of Gran Canaria.*

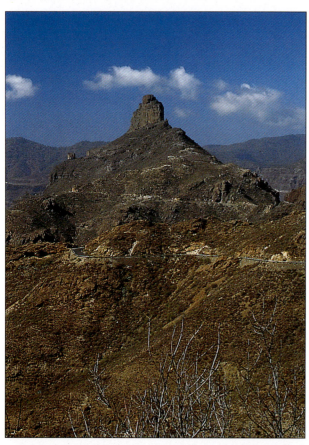

However, the effort involved in the ascent is amply compensated by the stupendous spectacle to be found: from the height of the peaks of Gran Canaria, beyond the veil of mist which gracefully softens the incredible transparency of the fresh air, a unique panorama can be enjoyed, where the eye can see beyond the neighboring peaks and embrace the deep blue of the ocean from which the shapes of the other islands of the archipelago emerge. An exploration of the highest peaks can also reserve some pleasant and unique surprises: from encounters with the last examples of the sea eagle and sparrowhawk who still live in the Canaries, to the discovery of the extraordinarily varied mountain flora. And from a height, the deep fractures in the *barrancos* can look like verdant fissures sliding silently down towards the sea.

This and following pages:
more extraordinarily evocative and, in some ways,
almost alpine views of the mountains on Gran Canaria:
vast stretches of conifers, of a characteristic dark green
color, which climb to the feet of the highest and
bleakest rocky peaks.

ARTENARA

Situated among the tall peaks, the small and ancient village of Artenara, the highest on the island with its altitude of 1250 m, and the most unique due to its primitive-style houses hollowed directly out of the stone, is notable for two particular attractions: the *Mesón de la Silla*, a restaurant created from the rock where it is possible to savor the tasty dishes of the local cuisine whilst admiring a breathtaking view of the *Roque Nublo* and *Roque Bentayga*; and the *Capilla della Virgen de la Cuevita*, hollowed out of the tuff, the destination every year on August 29th, of a crowded procession, with a torch-light procession at night.

Artenara, the highest town on the island, the famous Mesón de la Silla, a picturesque restaurant hollowed out of the rock.

Pinos de Gáldar, a volcanic depression surrounded by mountainous slopes, characterized by the presence of lavic rocks colonized by rich vegetation.

PINOS DE GÁLDAR

Along the road leading to Artenara, near Cruz de Tejeda, is situated the wide volcanic depression known as Pinos de Gáldar. This type of "natural" monument, where volcanic rocks are mingled with the lush surrounding vegetation creates one of the most outstanding features of the landscape to be seen at this point.

TELDE

This was the ancient capital of the Guanche civilization and is the second most important center of the whole island. It is characterized by the unmistakable features conferred upon it by the Spanish conquerors. In the **Iglesia de San Juan** (16th century), which is flanked by two identical modern bell-towers, a valuable series of Gothic sculptures (15th-16th centuries) can be seen.

Church of San Juan Bautista: a valuable Flemish altar-piece with Saint Gregory and Saint Francis is kept here (left) and a curious crucifix made of leaves and ears of corn set in an elaborate silver structure.

The marvelous church of San Juan Bautista, in Telde, situated between two twin towers.

INGENIO

Continuing southwards from Telde is Ingenio, whose name reminds us of what constituted for centuries, from the 16th century onwards, the true wealth of this area, the cultivation of sugar cane (*ingenios* in Spanish), and connected produce (mainly sugar and rum). In time, however, the economy of this small town of Portuguese origin which, today, has a population of over 25,000 inhabitants, has moved towards other products, and is now famous in particular for its excellent tomatoes, as well as straw hats and excellent locally produced needlework. In order to buy some particularly beautiful examples of this craft, one of the best places is the **Museo de Piedras y Artesanía Canaria**, just outside Ingenio, where it is also possible to admire a large amount of traditional agricultural equipment as well as a unique collection of rocks. Another striking feature of Ingenio is the presence, on the street corners, of the typical street sellers with *morenas*, large morays, which in these parts are considered to be a truly delicious dish.

The attractive white church of Ingenio and, below, the much visited Museo de Piedras y Artesanía Canaria, where it is possible to buy excellent needlework products and locally produced straw hats.

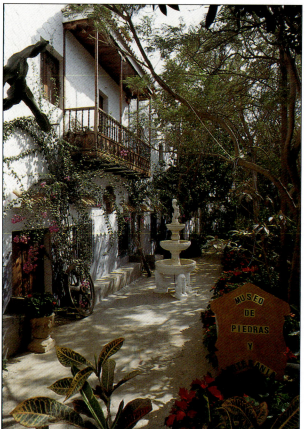

Some fascinating views of the steep walls of the Barranco de Guayadeque, studded with caves. A characteristic restaurant occupies one of the caves (top).

BARRANCO DE GUAYADEQUE

In the south-eastern area of the island of Gran Canaria, deeply wedged between the mountain slopes rising towards the *cumbre,* is the Barranco de Guayadeque. The dense collection of caves studding the cliffs which, for centuries, during the Guanche period, sheltered both men and goats, makes this one of the most exemplary *barrancos* of the island. Here, the natives put up a strenuous resistance to the Spanish conquest, and many of the mummies and ceramics now displayed in the Museo Canario in Las Palmas come from these rocks. In this area, which was the cradle of the Guanche culture, the first, famous and unmistakable *Tara idol* was found, and even today, it is still possible to experience the thrill of cave life by dining in a cave restaurant, situated actually inside the wall of the *barranco*: this is the only restaurant which still prepares a truly typical dish, *sancocho*, salted fish accompanied by sweet potatoes and *gofio* mixed with milk and bananas.

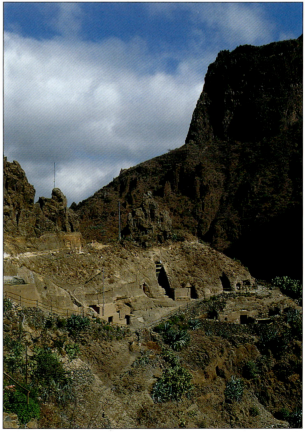

The earthenware of Gran Canaria

On Gran Canaria, the production of earthenware objects, which has long been the island's most widespread craft activity, can rightly be defined not only as being traditional, but even millenary, since it was inherited directly from the Guanche civilization. The production techniques also date back to the Guanche civilization and are still jealously preserved today and handed down by Canary Island craftsmen. In one place, the *Centro Locero de Lugarejo*, not far from Artenara, even the workshop where the earthenware is produced is the same one, suitably restored, where Guanche craftsmen worked centuries ago.

The basic raw materials used are clay (*barro*) and the so-called *arena negra de barranco*: the clay is extracted from walls of earth, dried, cleaned, left to deposit for a day in the water of the *pila del barro*, mixed with the *arena* and pugged until it is sufficiently pliable, then flattened out and rolled into *bastos*.

This paste is then shaped not with a wheel but directly by hand: in fact, a lump is taken which one hand revolves round slowly, whilst the other hand skillfully models it. Once the appearance of the object has been defined (whether this be a vase, bowl, plate, goblet or Tara idol), it must be left to dry for a couple of days and then freed (*raspado*) of impurities and imperfections (lumps of clay, small stones, etc.).

This earthenware is then given its characteristic red color by means of an operation called *teñido*: all or part of it is spread, still directly by hand, with the typical *almagra*, which has been extracted, dried, finely ground and then diluted with water.

The production of earthenware is one of the most ancient and traditional activities of Gran Canaria, rooted in the Guanche culture.

Once painted, the earthenware is decorated further with precise engravings carried out using a sort of punch, or *alisaderas*, and in some cases, colored black or green. In order for the objects to dry to perfection, after being exposed to the sun, the earthenware is actually cooked in a type of oven, the *guisadero*, fueled generally by the cones and branches of pine trees, as well as the many other types of trees and shrubs which grow on the slopes of these hills.

After being carefully *guisados*, the objects which are the fruit of this long working process, travel on towards the customary places of sale, bearing their cargo of history and tradition, ready to attract the attention and admiration of islanders and tourists with their rough charm.

From plates to vases, every type of earthenware object is rigorously modeled without the use of a wheel, by the craftsman's highly skilled hands. The decorative engravings are made with the use of special punches.

An exhaustive gallery of the simple but characteristic objects which constitute the typical earthenware production of Gran Canaria's craftsmen.
A collection of the various creations would not be complete without a reproduction of the famous and unmistakable Tara idol (top right).

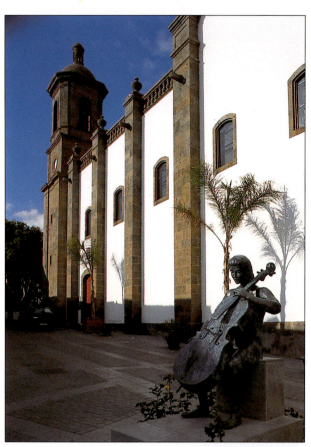

AGÜIMES

Just 3 Km away from Ingenio is Agüimes, for centuries a feud of the bishop of the Canaries, bestowed by King Ferdinand and Queen Isabella in gratitude for his contribution to the conquest of the archipelago. Even today, although the town has been free from this domination for over two centuries, the most conspicuous monuments are the marvelous *Bishop's Palace* and a *church* very similar to that of Ingenio. However, Agüimes is mainly famous for the big celebrations held during Carnival time, which is one of the most important events in island life, as well as, naturally, the important findings of Guanche remains, inscriptions and drawings discovered nearby (especially at *Temisa* and the *Barranco de Balos*).

The church of Agüimes, similar in every way to that of Ingenio except for the famous statue of a cellist erected at the side.

The pleasant village of Santa Lucía, lying between the green mountain slopes and the intense blue sky.

The striking exterior and two of the three rooms which make up La Fortaleza, an interesting ethnographic museum, Santa Lucía's pride and joy.

SANTA LUCÍA

Again located in the interior of the island, is the small but picturesque village of Santa Lucía, reclining in a natural green setting. However, the village's main attraction, in addition to its environmental qualities, is the interesting **Museo Etnográfico**, known as **La Fortaleza**, due to the appearance of the building in which it is housed: the result of the extraordinary passion of a local researcher, it is an extremely small museum (just three rooms), but exceptionally rich in valuable items, almost all finds dating back to the pre-Hispanic period.

ARTEDARA

A pleasant stay on the beaches of Maspalomas can be made even more interesting by a visit to the Guanche **necropolis** of Artedara, whose significant historical patrimony as well as the many discoveries made there, provide a stimulating look at the remote past of these lands. It can be reached by traveling towards the interior, between deep valleys and pronounced peaks, following a marvelous panoramic road leading up to the steep **valle de Fátaga**, where the necropolis is situated, through a region wrapped in an untamed charm, also due to the rough nature of the rocky land and the extreme "austerity" of the vegetation, which consists only of small palm groves and scanty groups of spurge, with occasional vast expanses of cultivated land.

Some characteristic examples of the complex earthenware production typical of the Guanche people, one of the last remaining records of this very interesting civilization. Note, below in the center, the famous and mysterious Tara idol.

Some fascinating panoramic views illustrating the wild and impervious natural conformation of the evocative Barranco de Fátaga, just a few kilometers into the interior from Maspalomas.

SAN AGUSTÍN

The features of the landscape on the southern side of Gran Canaria are in sharp contrast with the natural environment and the landscape of the territories of the northern regions. Its climatic, geographical and environmental features render this part of the island very similar to the north-west coast of Africa. In these regions the landscape takes on the typical features of a desert environment, with scarce vegetation, vast expanses of dunes which stretch down to the coast and even camels roaming around. However, over the last decades, the region has been heavily promoted and exploited as a tourist spot, with the result that, nowadays, the **southern coasts** of Gran Canaria have became the popular destination of a large flow of tourists who, mostly, come from Northern Europe.

The vast sea-front of San Agustín stretches along the coast for almost 15 kilometers, as far as the lighthouse situated at the extreme end of the coast of *Maspalomas*. The place grew up out of nothing and its modern and inviting features are characterized by large *hotel complexes*, numerous *residences*, *bungalows* and a great number of well-equipped tourist facilities. The wide beach along the sea-front which has fine golden sand, runs right down to the water's edge, beyond which lie the gently sloping shoals of the sea-bed. The exceptionally favorable climate present throughout the year, the brilliant sunshine and the crystal clear waters of the ocean are the main factors which have led to the place being a favorite tourist spot.

Top level tourist structures dot the famous southern coastal area of Gran Canaria.

Two views of the marvelous seaside resort of San Agustín, bordered by the outline of Punta Morro Besudo.

PLAYA DEL INGLÉS

The place is considered to be one of the most beautiful "pearls" in the long strand of coastal centers which overlook the shore facing the south coast of Gran Canaria. In fact, the picturesque *Punta de las Burras*, situated at the edge of a beach bearing the same name, divides the *Playa de San Agustín* from *Playa del Inglés*. This well-known resort is the most fashionable and trendy place on the Canaries. Its impressive growth, over the last decades, has led to hotels, residences, tourist apartment blocks, bungalows and rented facilities being constructed at a rate of almost mathematical progression. At the same time, all types of facilities catering for tourists and sightseers have been set up, giving visitors the possibility of being able to relax and enjoy themselves at the same time. Typical restaurants, shopping centers, night-clubs, discos, meeting places, swimming pools and a large wealth of sports facilities are on hand to provide recreation, sport and entertainment for the numerous foreign visitors who come here. It is not just a happy coincidence that most of the visitors come from Northern countries. In this fairy-tale oasis, amid the decorative green palm trees and thriving vegetation (cultivated by Man) the visitor comes across spacious avenues which stretch along the sea front with its bathing establishments and wide expanses of beaches.

Some views of the long, crowded beach which is one of the most popular attractions of Playa del Inglés.

MASPALOMAS

Maspalomas stretches out along the southernmost point of Gran Canaria and is, in fact, one of the most important tourist attractions on the whole island. Even though, up until a few years ago, the beaches of the "capital" of Las Palmas were considered to be the most important, attracting tourists from all over the world, the recent progressive rise in importance of the southern beaches has now put them in direct competition with the beaches and facilities of the main town of the island. Without doubt, it can be said that nowadays the southern beaches of Gran Canaria are definitely more fashionable and "trendy" than the once famous and exclusive ones of Las Palmas. Thanks to its exceptionally pleasant geographical position, located at the edge of a green oasis shaded by palm-trees and well irrigated by the fresh waters of a small lake, Maspalomas can be considered as being among the most important bathing resorts of Gran Canaria. Just outside the town, the landscape takes on a charming and almost dream-like quality,

because of the dunes which, driven by the wind, continually change shape and position creating the typically curious features of a desert landscape. Near the small lake, where a large quantity of hydrophilous plants thrive, many migrating birds can be seen. At the extreme end of the coast stands the unmistakable outline of the **Lighthouse**, whose warning signals are of primary importance for the ships which pass along the transoceanic routes.

The notable urban growth of this tourist center and holiday resort has led to the rise of modern and elegant residential complexes as well as hotels and holiday apartments. There are many facilities which provide entertainment, sporting activities and enjoyment for the visitors and tourists who come from all over Europe and more particularly from Northern countries. The hot sunshine of Maspalomas, the wide, pleasant beaches with their fine golden sands and finally the azure unpolluted sea water are just some of the attractions in great demand by the numerous foreign visitors who flock here.

On the following pages (88-89):
the vast expanse of sandy dunes, of an almost
African appearance, which attractively face the blue
stretch of sea behind Maspalomas.

One of the residences and tourist villages with
excellent facilities, the pride and joy of this famous
seaside resort.

The attractive white houses of Maspalomas.

On the previous pages (90-91):
more pictures of the immense desert-like expanses
where, on the background of a boundless marine
horizon, white tourist complexes can be seen, facing
onto beaches bordered with dunes.

These pages:
the peaceful dromedary remains one of
the favorite means of transport for
tourists who, high up on his back, can
explore the famous sandy expanses of
Maspalomas.

On the following pages: some ordinary views of
seaside life, under the slender shadow of the
famous Maspalomas lighthouse.

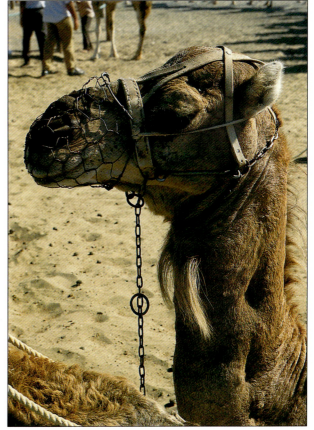

The success of Maspalomas' tourist industry is clearly witnessed by the imperious development of an up-to-date and well-equipped tourist complex, consisting of luxurious and comfortable hotels, top class restaurants, high level facilities and huge shopping malls (like the one shown on the opposite page, above). Amongst the most popular attractions is, without doubt, the famous sun center (top), where tourists can greatly benefit from a wise use of solar energy.

Palmitos Park

In the immediate vicinity of Maspalomas, is the truly delightful Palmitos Park, 200,000 square meters of luxuriant vegetation turned into a much visited nature park. Alongside the profuse local flora, it is possible to admire plants from every part of the world, which have become easily acclimatized due to the island's very favorable climate. To give an example, there are over 51 different types of palm trees, and over 230 different species of multi-colored tropical birds flying around this exuberant paradise, together with many colorful butterflies. Particular mention should also be made of the large expanses of cactus and marvelous stretches of orchids of the most varied forms and colors.

Palmitos Park is a true tropical paradise, particularly famous for its rich "collection" of cactuses. Amongst the park's guests, mention should certainly be made of the numerous species of birds, from parrots to pelicans, flamingos to the inevitable canaries, who brighten up the already idyllic atmosphere.

PARK

Some more glimpses of the thick and luxuriant vegetation which characterizes every corner of Palmitos Park, with cactuses, spurge, over fifty species of palm trees, orchids, small ponds with turtles and a myriad of multi-colored birds.

"Amagante" (Cistus symphytifolius). Easily recognised for the deep pink colour and size of its flowers, which can reach 5 centimetres in diameter, but the flowers of this cistus are extremely delicate and are easily damaged by a storm. Shrub reaching a metre in height with opposite, velvet-like leaves with prominent veins. Very common in the lower part of the altitudinal belt corresponding to pinewoods. An endemic to the Canary Islands.

Mundo Aborigen

"A day at the origins of a people" is offered by the unique Mundo Aborigen, located along the road which leads from *Playa del Inglés* to the *Barranco de Fátaga*. This is a fascinating natural size reconstruction of a typical Canary Island village before the Spanish conquest. Within an area of over 110,000 sq. m. in the heart of the *Ayaguares Nature Park*, just a few kilometers from Maspalomas, the various moments of the everyday life of the first inhabitants of the Canary Islands are illustrated with the help of a hundred or so perfectly reproduced human models. Probably of African origin, this people reached the archipelago between 2000 and 3000 BC, and remained its sole inhabitants until the end of the 14th century. This interesting park aims to highlight the high levels of civilization attained by these natives, better known as Guanches, who created substantial settlements, practiced agriculture and animal farming, but were also able to boast an excellent craft production and their own shrines. They also mummified the bodies of their deceased and had a precise social hierarchy, culminating in the *Guanartemes,* authentic kings of the island, and left us many significant examples of their artistic skills.

The faithful reconstructions with which Mundo Aborigen proposes to illustrate various moments in the everyday life of an ancient native village.

ARGUINEGUÍN

Arguineguín, which can be reached from Maspalomas, overlooks the south-western coast of Gran Canaria, at the opening of the valley which bears the same name, and is one of the most recently developed bathing resorts and tourist centers of the island. Its pleasant and sunny geographical position, overlooking the open sea, has led to the urbanization, in both tourist and residential terms, of the locality. Arguineguín has a small port where mainly fishing boats are berthed. During the day, these can usually be seen out at sea, as this stretch of water is particularly good for fishing.

A characteristic reconstruction of a Far West town, in the perfect setting of the rocks in the Cañón del Águila. This is where many feature and TV films are made, and it is possible to encounter numerous stunt men, testing their skills with lassos, pistols and knives.

A picture of the modern Aquasur Water Park.

A view of the fishing and tourist town of Arguineguín.

The welcoming seaside and residential facilities of the so-called Puesta de Sol.

PATALAVACA

The modern tourist settlement of Patalavaca is in fact a residential area which stands almost next door to Arguineguín. The place has a small, pretty beach with fine golden sands and is known as *Playa de la Verga*. The features of the modern tourist complexes and residential blocks of flats have been inspired by the linear, futuristic styles of modern architecture. There are numerous spots shaded by palm trees, where tourists can enjoy the benefits of the extraordinary climate of the Canaries.

The futuristic residential complexes of Patalavaca which, with their elegant swimming pools, luxuriant gardens and elaborate facilities, directly overlook the seashore.

PUERTO RICO

The charming coastal resort of Puerto Rico faces the south-western coastal front of Gran Canaria, close to the cape from which it gets its name. The origins of this resort, like many other centers along the southern coast, are linked to the relatively recent developments in tourism. The modern bold architectural features of the residences, hotels and residential blocks of flats are contained within a landscape and environment of great natural beauty. Puerto Rico has first-class facilities and offers numerous opportunities for recreation and sports activities. In the small functional tourist port, many boats belonging to sailing enthusiasts are moored.

A splendid view of Puerto Rico, lying in a stupendous inlet, with the much visited tourist marina and the white shapes of the residential complexes and elegant condominiums which overlook the luxuriant vegetation.

TAURITO

Taurito is a recently developed tourist center, where building work on tourist accommodation facilities is still under way. It lies at the opening of a wide valley close to the *Playa de Tauro*. This bathing resort is yet another link along the chain of coastal settlements which have risen up, as if by magic, along the south-western coast of the island. Here too, the modern linear features of its architecture are pleasantly situated against the natural background of the landscape of Gran Canaria.

The attractive sea belvedere of Taurito.

A modern hotel in the famous seaside resort with its elegant swimming pool.

Two images which illustrate the precious results of the considerable tourist urbanization work carried out.

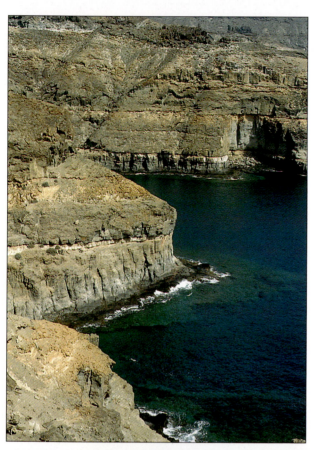

Characteristic Features of the South-Western Coast

T he varied morphology and structure of the island of Gran Canaria, has led to its being known, with good reason, as a "miniature continent". An example which has given rise to this assertion can be seen along the southern coast where, against a background rich in landscape and environmental features, the tourist can, every now and again, catch glimpses of varied and enchanting views. In this way, one can note the differences between the desert-like, flat and sandy coast of San Agustín, the coast of Maspalomas characterized by its dunes which slope down towards the sea, and the beaches located along the openings of the steep mountain valleys of Arguineguín, Puerto Rico and Taurito. Farther along, the south-west coast becomes high and rocky, with steep cliffs which descend vertically down to the sea, where a setting of great natural beauty is created by the composite nature of volcanic rocks and the majestic spectacle of the waves which break against the rugged and winding cliffs.

Some characteristic aspects of the south-western coast, where the high rocky offshoots (left, Barranco del Taurito, opposite page, below, Punta del Baso de la Arena), with their unique lavic rock formations (opposite page, top left), alternate with vast stretches of sandy dunes.

PLAYA DE LOS AMADORES

In the wonderful Puerto Rico area, one of the last beaches to be discovered by the tourist industry, despite a natural setting of charming beauty and a particularly transparent sea, Playa de los Amadores is a white strip of sand stretching along a small inlet beyond *Punta de Puerto Rico* and *Punta de la Hondura*. Undoubtedly, the proximity to a famous seaside resort like Puerto Rico has favored the rapid success of the wonderful Playa de los Amadores, where the tourist structures have had to (and managed to) adapt themselves in order to meet the large and continually growing demands of the tourist industry.

PUERTO MOGÁN

Puerto Mogán is practically the last center along the south-west coast of the island and is situated at the opening of the *valley of Mogán*, across which runs a road which leads up to the town bearing the same name. The small coastal center is believed to be among the main fishing ports of the island and offers its visitors views of decidedly modern buildings which are clearly influenced by the characteristic features of Spanish architecture. One of the outstanding characteristics of the place is that it has managed to maintain the dimensions which make it a comfortable place to live in, even in these modern times.

Opposite page: a characteristic image of Puerto Mogán, with its white houses mirrored in the sea waters.

On the following pages: the tourist marina at Puerto Mogán.

A view of the Playa de los Amadores, one of the latest places to be exploited for tourism.

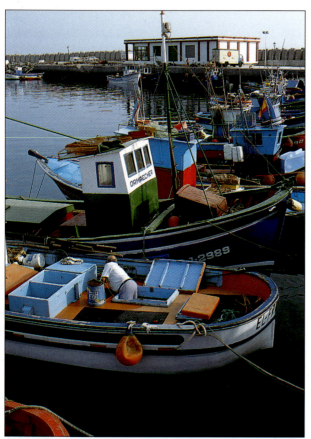

The features of Puerto Mogán are in striking contrast with the modern and gaudy architecture of the other coastal centers along the southern side of Gran Canaria. Here, at Puerto Mogán, the small spacious plazas are shaded by palm-trees, while the roads and lanes - fortunately free of traffic - are all clean and neat, and the white fronts of the houses, decorated with small balconies, are connected to each other by pretty stone arches. The houses are dominated by sunny terraces along which grow plants and small trees and upon which stand pretty and decorative pergolas. Along the quays and wharves of the port, the fishermen carry out their tasks in silent tranquillity, while the glowing colors of the fishing boats and numerous other craft moored here, are picturesquely reflected in the crystal waters of the sea.

More small craft anchored at Puerto Mogán.

The typical architectural style of Puerto Mogán, with the unique little houses, distinguished by their elegant pergolas and the enchanting recurring theme of ornamental arches which connect the individual buildings to each other.

F L O R A

The archipelago of the Canary Islands lies in the Atlantic Ocean, 100 kilometres west of the Moroccan coast. The oldest islands are those nearest the African Coast, whilst leaving the coast and proceeding seaward the islands are of increasingly recent formation. From East to West, the sea surrounding the islands also becomes deeper; the depth of the sea is about 1,000 metres between the African coast and Lanzarote but 4,000 metres off La Palma. Consequently, proceeding from East to West, the archipelago gains more and more oceanic characteristics whilst losing its continental ones. Because of this peculiar geographical position, types of tropical and subtropical vegetation have managed to survive which once also occurred within the Mediterranean Basin but which disappeared after two major catastrophes. The first was the desertification in the late Miocene (Messiniano 8-9 million years ago) as a result of the orogenesis of the mountain chain corresponding to the Atlas Mountains and the Sierra Nevada of today, a phenomenon which brought a lower water supply from the Atlantic and consequently a drier and cooler climate to the surrounding lands. This was followed by a series of glacial cycles during the interval between the Pliocene and Pleistocene (1.5-0.1 million years ago) which cooled the land over the entire northern hemisphere with the consequent disappearance from Southern Europe and the Mediterranean lands of those subtropical types which had managed to survive the events of the Miocene. Other islands in the Atlantic Ocean also experienced these geological phenomena: the Azores, Madeira, the Salvajes Islands and Capoverde, which, together with the Canaries, form the biogeographical region known as Macaronesia. When the first people to visit the "Lucky Archipelago" saw the fire and smoke exuding from Teide, they called Tenerife "The Island of Hell". Fortunately this name did not pass into history, nor is there any record of it on the geographical maps. Its present name seems to be linked to a poem by Viana, who described the mountain as "tener-ife" - the mountain with snow. Snow and fire are in fact the two extremes which characterise the entire archipelago and testify the almost double nature of the Canaries. Indeed, the marked altitudinal range of the volcanoes are responsible for the great climatic contrasts typical of these islands.

The wet, cool air currents from the West and North-west, the Trade Winds, bring a cool wet, typically oceanic climate to the windward slopes of the islands, favouring a hardy and luxuriant vegetation. Altitudes between 300 and 1,500 metres feel the effect of the Trade Winds the most; below this level their effect is only slight, whilst over this altitude they are almost negligible and the climate is dry with very hot summers and harsh winters. The slopes facing Africa are not only excluded from the benefits of the Trade Winds, which die out on the western slopes, they also feel the influence of the hot and dry winds blowing from the Sahara and are thus extremely dry. These marked climatic contrasts have favoured the islands' rich biodiversity.

Man's agricultural exploitation of the Canaries has undoubtedly been influenced by this situation. No certain data are available about who were the first people to colonise the islands, but in all probability the first settlers had North African somatic characters and they are known as the Guanches or Canarios. They had a Neolithic type of culture, so lived by simple sustainable agriculture and certainly in harmony with nature. Phoenicians, Persians and Carthaginians probably landed on the island in about 500 BC, but Pliny the Elder was the first to tell about an expedition to the "Lucky Islands" by Juba, Prince of Mauretania in the times of the Emperor Augustus. During the late Middle Ages, ships from Genoa and Majorca reached the islands, with Fernandez de Lugo as captain under the service of the Catholic Kings, who at the end of 1496 finally conquered the islands and incorporated them in the Crown of Castilla. The lands were divided and thus the transformation of the vegetation and landscape of the archipelago first began. The islands underwent massive deforestation to make room for growing cereals, in particular, sugar cane, vineyards, and orchards which flourished on the wet slopes where conditions were ideal for their cultivation. On the higher slopes, agriculture gave way to grazing, which exerted strong pressure on the autoctonous floral heritage.

With the increase in transatlantic traffic, the Canaries became a compulsory port of call for ships on their way to Spain from Latin America. Many species of exotic plants, both alimentary and ornamental, broke their journey on the archipelago, which thus became a sort of acclimatising garden. As a result, many species from Central and Southern America became part of the local flora, sometimes even taking its place. At present there are as many as 500 species of naturalised exotic flora in the Canaries, many of which live in areas of human settlement.

Over the last few years, traditional methods of agriculture have been abandoned and man-built spaces have increased. With the expansion of towns and industry and growing demographic pressures, linked especially with the tourist industry, the environment has deteriorated badly. The expansion of man-centred interests over the natural heritage, like the construction of roads, has seriously cut down the amount of the ecosystems originally present in the archipelago to just 20% of the total surface area.

The first important contribution to the knowledge of the natural heritage of these islands was the treatise by Webb & Berthelot. P.B. Webb (1793-1854) was a rich English landowner whose love of botany led him to travel the world. On his journey from Madeira to Brazil, in 1828 he stopped at Tenerife where he met S. Berthelot (1794-1880), who had already been collecting insects and plants of the islands for some years.

At present, the flora of the Canary Islands consists of approximately 2,000 species, 520 of which can be considered endemic and as many as 593 rare or under threat of extinction.

"Alpinia zerumbet"
flowers the whole year through. Originally from South-east Asia.

LAVANDULA CANARIENSIS MILL. ▼

(Labiatae) Hierba del risco

Endemic species to the Canary Islands, this shrub is woody at the base with erect herbaceous branches, ending in inflorescences. Opposite, pubescent and pinnate leaves, green-greyish in colour with rounded lateral appendices. Violet flowers gathered in long, spiked and branched inflorescences.

ISOPLEXIS CANARIENSIS (L.) LOUD. ▲

(Scrophulariaceae) Crista de Gallo

A perennial figwort with woody base up to a metre high. Lanceolate, coriaceous and slightly pubescent leaves. Large flowers (about 3 centimetres long), bright red-orange arranged in dense inflorescences. *I. canariensis* is endemic to the Canary Islands. On Gran Canaria a further two species occur, *I. isabelliana* (Webb & Berth.) Masf. and *I. chalcantha* Svent. & O'Shan.

ARTEMISIA THUSCULA CAV. ▲

(Compositae) Ajenjo

Small shrub easily recognised by the strong smell of incense the leaves give when they are rubbed. Reaching up to a metre in height, the leaves are a silver grey colour and usually flaccid. Flowers in small, golden-yellow, very compact inflorescences. *A. thuscula* is endemic to the Canary Islands.

◄ LAVANDULA BUCHII WEBB

(Labiatae) Mato risco

Easily recognised both by is pale blue to violet flowers and for its pinnate leaves covered by a thick and dense layer of hairs, giving it a greyish hue and a cotton like touch. It differs from the other species of the genus *Lavandula* found on the Canaries on account of its hairy leaves and its calyx which is longer than the underlying bracts.

LAVATERA ACERIFOLIA CAV. ▶

(Malvaceae) Malva silvestre

Species endemic to the Canary Islands, distinguished from the rarer *L. phoenicea* Vent. by its flowers which are darker and narrower at the base. A shrub up to 2.5 metres high with large, palmate leaves with irregularly toothed lobes and very long petiole. Flowers large (up to 7-8 centimetres in diameter), mauve, darker at the base, rarely whitish in colour.

DRACAENA DRACO
(L.) L.
(Dracaenaceae) Drago

A tree-like plant with massive, short thick trunk which divides into a series of almost dichotomous branches, each carrying a tuft of leaves in a rosette at the tip. The leaves are linear, rigid, green-grey in colour and up to 60 centimetres long in large specimens. Small, whitish flowers gathered in a drooping inflorescence. Round, fleshy, orange coloured fruits. The plant is an endemic of the Macaronesian Islands. There are many legends attached to the "Canaries Dragon": mediaeval manuscripts narrate that the blood-red lymph, or "sangre de dragón", which escapes when the bark is cut, is magical and endowed with medical properties capable of curing ulcers and dysentery. There has been a lot of speculation as to how long a Dracena can live: Alexander von Humboldt, one of the earliest explorers of the Canary Islands, tells that a plant in the Orotava Valley which was destroyed by a hurricane in 1867, was more

than 6,000 years old. Fenzl, in an article in the "Gardener's Chronicle", writes that the circumference of the same plant reached 78 feet (27 metres). Along with the Canary Palm, it only grows wild in some particular areas where a few individuals occur which differ somewhat from those commonly seen at Icod de los Vinos. *D. draco* can be considered a living fossil and is therefore a protected species in the habitat where it occurs spontaneously.

Perennial herbaceous plant with woody base. Leaves organised in a large basal rosette which can reach up to a metre in diameter. Tomentose, pinnate leaves with sharp tip. Floral scape can reach a metre and a half in height; the composite inflorescences carried at the top are characteristic because they are sheathed by white, hairy bracts. Species endemic to the Canary Islands.

MAYTENUS CANARIENSIS ►
(LOES.) KUNK. & SUND.
(Celastraceae) Perarillo

Small tree no higher than 7-8 metres, which in rocky, cliff-like places takes on the form of a prostrate shrub. Irregular trunk with dark, very rough bark, short, knotted and crooked branches, crown small and sparse. Shiny green, long-lasting leaves with short petiole, ovate blade and toothed edges. Small, white flowers in axillary clusters high on the branches. The fleshy fruits are divided into three valves. Endemic species to the Canaries.

◄ *VIBURNUM TINUS* **L. SUBSP.**
RIGIDUM **(VENT.) P.SILVA**
(Caprifoliaceae) Afollado

Typical shrub of the laurel wood underbrush, its presence is a sign of good conservation of the tree layer since it does not like much light. Up to 5-6 metres high, the young branches are hairy. Large, opposite leaves (up to 20 centimetres long and 12 centimetres wide), very hairy and sometimes bristly and reddish when still young. Small, white and perfumed flowers arranged in rich end inflorescences. Endemic to the Canaries and can be used as an ornamental tree for gardens and hedges as long as in the shade.

◀ *PINUS CANARIENSIS*
CHR.SM. EX DC.
(Pinaceae) Pino canario

Can be a large tree (some specimens are known to reach 60 m in height and have a trunk over 2.5 m in diameter). Needle-like leaves, sometimes pale green, reaching 30 centimetres in length and arranged in tufts of three. Straight trunk, bark a grey colour with grey-reddish plates. The "Canary Pine" is endemic to the archipelago, but it only grows wild at Tenerife, La Palma, Gran Canaria and Hierro; reports for La Gomera refer to specimens introduced by man.

FEIJOA SELLOWIANA ▶
O.BERG.
(Myrtaceae)

A shrub reaching approximately 6 metres in height characterised by tomentum-covered branches. The leaves are persistent, opposite, bi-coloured with the upper page dark green and the lower tomentose. Single flowers, with purple interior and tomentose exterior. Edible fruits tasting like Pineapple. In the wild it is widespread in Southern Brazil, Paraguay and Argentina.

SONCHUS CANARIENSIS (SCH.BIP.) BOULOS
(Compositae) Cerraja arborea

Belongs to the arboreal *Sonchus* group (*Dendrosonchus* section), of which it is the largest. Shrub consisting of an erect stem, straight or with two or three ramifications, each bearing a rosette of leaves at the tip, similar to that carried by the herbaceous *Sonchus* at ground level. The stem, in this case, reaches 3 meters in height. Leaves pinnate, toothed, up to 15-20 centimetres long. The inflorescences are carried on one or two branches which leave the centre of the rosette, each of which can bear up to 100-150 little yellow-coloured composite inflorescences. Endemic to the Canaries.

CAMPYLANTHUS SALSOLOIDES (L. FIL.) ROTH
(Scrophulariaceae) Romero marino

Shrub up to 2 metres tall. Leaves linear and succulent. Flowers varying in colour from pink to pale blue to whitish and arranged in loose inflorescences, sometimes curved. An endemic plant to the Canaries.

CHAMAECYTISUS PROLIFERUS (L. FIL.) LINK
(Leguminosae) Escobón

Bush branched from the base, up to 4 metres tall, sometimes reaching 7. Trunk with dark grey bark. Trifoliate, greyish green leaves carried on a petiole more or less the same length as the leaves. White flowers borne on the highest portions of the branches. Fruits are pods up to 7 centimetres long. The species is very variable and some varieties have been recognised which do not seem to depend on ecological conditions.

ECHIUM ACULEATUM POIR.
(Boraginaceae) Taginaste

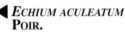

Small tree up to 3 metres high, with a short trunk and roundish branched crown. The leaves are linear and tend to be carried high near the flowers. Pale blue to white flowers gathered in short, spiked inflorescences. Endemic to the Canaries, but absent from Lanzarote and Fuerteventura.

Euphorbia canariensis L. ▶
(Euphorbiaceae) Cardon

The most characteristic plant of the hot dry habitat in the lower areas of the Canary Islands. A small tree, up to 3-4 metres tall, with succulent, green cactus-like trunk, square or pentagonal in section. The leaves are transformed into thorns, up to 5-14 millimetres long and arranged in tufts of three or four. The flowers are a green to red colour. An endemic species to the Canaries but rare in the eastern islands.

Euphorbia obtusifolia ▶
Poir.
(Euphorbiaceae) Tabaiba amarga

Like the other species of the genus *Euphorbia* which can be found in the driest parts of the Canaries, *E. obtusifolia* is a small tree characterised by the short, always well evident trunk and by a wide, almost round crown with branches that carry the leaves in tufts at the tip. A common plant, especially in the hottest and driest areas, up to 2 meters high with upright trunk. Leaves linear, with sharp tip, up to 7 centimetres long and no more than 6 millimetres wide. Flowers arranged in inflorescences called cyathiums, with pale green bracts. This species is distributed in North Africa and the Canaries.

INDEX

Introduction .... page   3
History .... ”   4

LAS PALMAS .... ”   7
- Calle Mayor .... ” 20
- Casa de Colón .... ” 22
- Castillo de la Luz .... ” 11
- Catedral de Santa Ana .... ” 28
- Diocesan Museum of Sacred Art .... ” 31
- "El Bodegón" .... ” 19
- Home-Museum of Benito Pérez Galdós .... ” 21
- Museo de Néstor .... ” 17
- Parque de Santa Catalina .... ” 14
- Parque Doramas .... ” 15
- Parque San Telmo .... ” 20
- Playa de las Canteras .... ” 12
- Plaza del Cairasco .... ” 32
- Port, The .... ” 10
- Pueblo Canario .... ” 17

Agüimes .... ” 78
Arguineguín .... ” 105
Artedara .... ” 80
Artenara .... ” 68
ARUCAS .... ” 36
Balcón de Zamora .... ” 55
Barranco de Guayadeque .... ” 73
Caldera de Bandama .... ” 48
Cenobio de Valerón .... ” 38

Characteristic Features
    of the South-Western Coast .... page 112
Cruz de Tejeda .... ” 56
Earthenware of Gran Canaria, The .... ” 74
Gáldar .... ” 42
Great mountains, The .... ” 58
Guía .... ” 42
Ingenio .... ” 72
Jardín Canario .... ” 46
MASPALOMAS .... ” 86
Mundo Aborigen .... ” 102
Palmitos Park .... ” 98
Patalavaca .... ” 106
Pinos de Gáldar .... ” 69
Playa de los Amadores .... ” 114
PLAYA DEL INGLÉS .... ” 85
PUERTO DE LAS NIEVES .... ” 45
Puerto Mogán .... ” 114
PUERTO RICO .... ” 108
SAN AGUSTÍN .... ” 82
San Mateo .... ” 48
Santa Lucía .... ” 79
Taurito .... ” 110
Telde .... ” 70
TEROR .... ” 50
- Basílica de la Virgen del Pino .... ” 53
Typical Features
    of the Northern Side of the Island .... ” 34

FLORA .... ” 120